Copyright © 2024 by Mentors Care. All rights reserved.

This publication is meant as a source of valuable information for the reader, however it is not meant as a substitute for direct expert assistance. If such a level of assistance is required, the services of a competent professional should be sought.

DEAR MENTOR,

I see you.
I value you.
I appreciate you.

Thank you for stepping forward to support a student.

I understand that not every day or every encounter will be an easy one. Our intention with this guide is to help you feel supported, especially on those tough days.

Sometimes, students may initially lack manners or respect. They may say things that downright shock you. But know that your unconditional love—meeting them where they are, without judgment, and creating a safe space—will make a significant difference in their lives. I've witnessed this time and time again since founding Mentors Care in 2009.

This guide, along with your annual training and grade-specific Talking Points® booklet, will provide you with the tools to build a strong relationship with your student while also caring for your own well-being. When combined with support from your on-site Mentors Care coordinator, you'll have a well-rounded resource bank so you, too, feel cared for.

Even with all of this, we know that there is always room for improvement.

In the words of Coach Vince Lombardi, *"Perfection is not attainable, but if we chase perfection, we can catch excellence."* We'll continue to strive for excellence and know that you will, too.

With a grateful heart,

DENA PETTY
Founder, Mentors Care

VISTRA

AT VISTRA, WE CARE about the communities we serve. It's one of our core principles and part of our mission to support meaningful change for the next generation of Texans – change that often starts in school.

That's why we're proud to help sustain Mentors Care and its work to help high school students succeed. Issues like homelessness and poverty are challenging enough for adults to overcome and can often shape the trajectory of a child's life. But **never underestimate the difference one person can make.**

By serving as a mentor, you're providing more than just guidance and life experience. You're inspiring these students and helping them see what's possible.

Investing in Mentors Care is an investment in the future. Struggling students understand they're not alone to face life's challenges. That someone truly cares for them. That they matter.

Thank you for joining our mission to power a better way forward.

ANNETTE UNDERWOOD
Chief Diversity Officer, Vistra Corp.

TABLE OF CONTENTS

INTRODUCTION — 7

PART ONE: POLICIES, PROCEDURES, & GUIDELINES

1.1 Advocating for Your Mentee — 10
1.2 Discipline — 10
1.3 Displays of Affection — 10
1.4 Exchange of Phone Numbers — 12
1.5 Frequency of Meetings — 13
1.6 Meeting Places — 13
1.7 Mentee Family Contact — 14
1.8 Mentee Social Emotional Safety & Wellbeing — 14
1.9 Transportation Issues — 14
1.10 Virtual Meetings — 15

PART TWO: RESOURCES, TOOLS, & ACTIVITIES TO SUPPORT YOU

2.1 Mentoring Realities — 18
2.2 Your Role as a Mentor — 20
2.3 Understanding Defense Mechanisms — 23
2.4 Boundary Setting — 27
2.5 Five Step Reflection on Rough Visits — 30
2.6 Processing Feelings of Rejection — 33
2.7 Twelve Stages of Burnout — 35
2.8 Five Types of Imposter Syndrome — 36
2.9 Success Stories to Fuel You — 38

PART THREE: RESOURCES, TOOLS, & ACTIVITIES TO SUPPORT YOUR MENTEES

- 3.1 About the Talking Points® — 46
- 3.2 The CARE Model — 47
- 3.3 Showing Up For Your Student — 50
- 3.4 Five Conversation Types for Mentors — 52
- 3.5 Feelings Wheel (abbreviated version) — 53
- 3.6 Conversation Tools for Common Teen Issues — 54
    - Depression — 54
    - Anxiety — 55
    - Grief — 56
    - Self-Harm — 57
    - Eating Disorders — 58
    - Substance Abuse — 59
    - Bullying/Cyberbullying — 60
    - Trauma — 61
- 3.7 Engagement/Relationship Building Activities & Games — 62
    - Mentors Care Uno® — 62
    - Would You Rather… — 64
    - Desert Island Game — 69
    - Shopping Spree Game — 71
    - Timeline of Me — 74
    - Open Ended Questions — 76

RESOURCES QUICK REFERENCE GRID — 79

RESOURCES TO-GO — 80

ACKNOWLEDGMENTS — 81

INTRODUCTION

YOU ARE PROOF that mentors care. It's more than a slogan; it's a fact.

We care, too. That's why we've created this guide for you. It's designed to provide support on multiple levels.

In Part 1, you'll find policies, guidelines, and legal requirements relevant to your role as a mentor available at your fingertips.

In Part 2, we shift our focus to providing resources that support you as a whole person.

In Part 3, a variety of tools and resources are available to help you foster relationships with your mentee.

As useful as we believe you'll find all this to be, it's important to note that this is not an exhaustive list of tools and resources.

For this guide, we've included items that we expect to remain relevant over time, while also providing a growing bank of digital resources accessible by scanning a QR code at the end of the book—resources that 'meet the moment,' addressing trending issues, challenges, and newly available tools.

We also want to emphasize that beyond these pages and the digital resources, your most important lifeline will always be your Mentors Care Coordinator. Many Mentors Care coordinators are licensed social workers, former teachers, former youth pastors and all receive special training to keep them up-to-date on legal requirements as well as emerging trends. They are the liaison between you and your mentee and between students and the school as well as students and professional referrals within the community.

You'll hear us mention this on multiple occasions because they are a tremendous asset for you, mentees, and the ongoing success of our organization.

As you review each section ahead, know that this is not a book that you'll read cover-to-cover once but a pocket style guide that you can come back to time and time again. Everyone will use it slightly differently; focus on the way it works best for you.

Onward!

PART ONE

Policies, Procedures, & Guidelines

ABOUT THIS SECTION

While you will review and recertify on up-to-date policies, procedures, and guidelines annually, we're providing a few for you here for your quick reference. As always, if you have any questions or concerns, please do not hesitate to contact your coordinator.

1.1 ADVOCATING FOR YOUR MENTEE

Mentors Care has agreements with the schools it serves, which obligates it and its mentors to follow its rules and regulations. Due to FERPA laws, the parent/guardian has legal rights as to the student's education. We are given access only to grades and attendance with the permission of the parent/guardian. As a Mentors Care mentor, <u>you cannot act as an advocate in communication with the school staff and administration.</u>

But if you feel that attention needs to be brought to the appropriate staff or administration, you can inform the coordinator and they will navigate appropriate avenues to help the student. *You are an advocate, in that you bring important information to the Mentors Care coordinator that would assist the student in a more successful education.*

1.2 DISCIPLINE

Mentors should never scold or otherwise attempt to discipline mentees, whether verbally or otherwise.

1.3 DISPLAYS OF AFFECTION

Many of our participating students have been abused in one way or another by adults in their lives. It is important that they not be confused or feel threatened by anything you might do in your role as their mentor.

As such, Mentors Care mentors should not hug mentees or touch them in any way that might cause them to feel uncomfortable or threatened, or that might otherwise be regarded by anyone (including without limitation, the mentees, other students, their parents, teachers, and school administrators, Mentors Care, and/or local law enforcement) as being inappropriate; regardless of whether your conduct in doing so might appear to be welcomed by the mentee at the time.

Limit any physical contact to handshakes, fist bumps, and/or pats on the back only.

INAPPROPRIATE CONDUCT ON THE PART OF MENTORS WILL NOT BE TOLERATED.

MENTORS SHOULD UNDERSTAND THAT :

(1) ANY AND ALL ALLEGATIONS OF SEXUAL MISCONDUCT OR PHYSICAL ABUSE OF ANY KIND MUST BE REPORTED TO LOCAL LAW ENFORCEMENT FOR FURTHER INVESTIGATION, AND

(2) EVEN A COMPLETELY FALSE AND/OR UNSUBSTANTIATED ALLEGATION OF SEXUAL MISCONDUCT OR PHYSICAL ABUSE ON THE PART OF A MENTOR CAN EXPOSE A MENTOR TO PUBLIC RIDICULE, INVESTIGATION, AND/OR ARREST. IN LIGHT OF THE FOREGOING, MENTORS SHOULD USE THEIR UTMOST AND BEST JUDGMENT WHEN DEALING WITH MENTEES, AND NOT ENGAGE IN ANY CONDUCT THAT MIGHT POSSIBLY BE

REGARDED AS BEING UNLAWFUL OR INAPPROPRIATE, REGARDLESS OF THE PURITY OF THE MENTOR'S MOTIVATIONS OR INTENTIONS.

1.4 EXCHANGE OF PHONE NUMBERS

You may share phone numbers with your mentee if you are comfortable in doing so, but Mentors Care discourages you from doing so.

Mentors Care prefers that you limit your communication with your mentee to a text if you share your phone number so that there is always documentation of your contact.

IF YOU CHOOSE TO SHARE YOUR PHONE NUMBER WITH YOUR MENTEE OR OTHERWISE COMMUNICATE WITH ANY MENTEE IN ANY SETTING OTHER THAN A GROUP SETTING AT WHICH THE PROGRAM COORDINATOR IS PRESENT, BE AWARE THAT YOUR CONDUCT IN DOING SO MAY OPEN THE DOOR TO POSSIBLE ALLEGATIONS OF MISCONDUCT OR INAPPROPRIATE BEHAVIOR THAT MAY BE MORE DIFFICULT TO DISPROVE OR REFUTE, AND WHICH MIGHT OTHERWISE HAVE NEVER ARISEN HAD YOU ONLY COMMUNICATED WITH YOUR MENTEE IN A GROUP SETTING INSTEAD.

1.5 FREQUENCY OF MEETINGS

You will be scheduled to meet with your mentee for one hour, once a week for about 26 weeks during the school year. You will not meet during the school holidays or the summer. It is *VERY* important to communicate with the Mentors Care Coordinator if you cannot meet during your scheduled time. (You can also let your mentee know, but first, contact the Coordinator to ease confusion.) They will be happy to reschedule your time and let your student know you are not meeting. **When you do not show up without communication, many will think that you do not like them.**

1.6 MEETING PLACES

You cannot meet your mentee outside of school and may only meet with your mentee during scheduled meetings set up by the Mentors Care coordinator. During your scheduled time, we ask that you find a setting where you and your mentee can speak in confidence, but which is always in clear view of the public.

Visits to your home in any way are expressly prohibited. You should never meet with a mentee in any location other than a group meeting or group setting which is hosted, sponsored, or otherwise supervised by one or more Program Coordinators for Mentors Care.

1.7 MENTEE FAMILY CONTACT

We ask that you HAVE NO CONTACT with the family of your mentee. If you feel that this is necessary to best help your mentee with a situation, you must talk to the Mentor Care coordinator about the issue.

1.8 MENTEE SOCIAL EMOTIONAL SAFETY & WELLBEING

Although confidentiality is important between mentor and mentee, claims of abuse, thoughts of suicide, reports serious physical or emotional health issues must be reported to the Mentors Care Coordinator.

The mentee will have already been made aware during their intake interview, that the law requires Mentors Care and its mentors to report claims of abuse and thoughts of suicide.

If a mentee ever tells you they're thinking about killing themself or are otherwise having thoughts of suicide, tell them to hang up and call 911, and to then stay on the line with the 911 operator until help arrives. *You are a mentor, not a first responder.*

1.9 TRANSPORTATION ISSUES

You must never be present with a mentee in an automobile, whether the automobile is moving or not, and must not transport or travel with a mentee under any circumstance, regardless of the mode of transportation or whether the destination is across the street, across town or across the country. Unfortunately, many of our participating students have little access to transportation to take care of life situations outside of school. If you know of a need, please bring this to the attention of the Mentors Care coordinator.

1.10 VIRTUAL MEETINGS

Virtual meetings should only occur using Microsoft Team Meetings conducted through Mentors Care's Teams Platform Microsoft Corporation is generously providing Mentors Care with access to and use of Microsoft Teams, which is a secure, online platform that allows users to conduct virtual meetings through their computers using the Internet. As a mentor, this platform will allow you to safely and securely meet with your mentee "virtually" as opposed to in person, by creating a secure "Team" that is configured by Mentors Care with the help of Microsoft's continuing support and related services, and then allowing users to connect with other on the "Mentors Care Team".

This platform will also enable Mentors Care to monitor and record all interactions between mentors and their mentees. Virtual meetings conducted through Mentors Care Team are subject to the same guidelines, norms and restrictions as otherwise apply to face-to-face meetings, and all meetings are electronically recorded to ensure compliance.

BE ADVISED THAT ALL VIRTUAL MEETINGS BETWEEN MENTORS AND MENTEES WHICH ARE CONDUCTED THROUGH THE USE OF MENTORS CARE'S MICROSOFT TEAM PLATFORM WILL BE RECORDED AND ARE SUBJECT TO MONITORING BY MENTORS CARE, WITHOUT FURTHER NOTICE OR CONSENT ON THE PART OF THE PARTICIPANTS.

BY YOUR CONDUCT IN USING THIS PLATFORM, YOU CONSENT TO MENTORS CARE'S MONITORING AND RECORDING OF ALL VIRTUAL MEETINGS AND AGREE TO BE BOUND BY SUCH TERMS AND CONDITIONS AS MICROSOFT CORPORATION AND/OR MENTORS CARE MAY PRESCRIBE.

MENTORS MUST NOT "FACETIME" WITH THEIR MENTEE OR OTHERWISE MEET WITH THEIR MENTEE VIRTUALLY, THROUGH THE USE OF ZOOM OR ANY OTHER VIRTUAL MEETING PLATFORM, EXCEPT FOR THE MENTORS CARE TEAM PLATFORM HOSTED BY MICROSOFT CORPORATION.

PART TWO

Resources, Tools, & Activities to Support You

ABOUT THIS SECTION

What you are doing is hard and we do not want you to feel alone. In addition to your Mentors Care coordinator and the entire Mentors Care staff, we're providing the resources in this section to prepare and equip you with tools to help manage expectations, set boundaries, and take good care of yourself as you enter your mentoring journey.

2.1 MENTORING REALITIES

You are so incredibly important in the life of your student even *if they do not show you.*

You are important to us, too.

Persistent support can spark transformation, but the road to lasting change is often filled with setbacks and challenges. Understanding this will help you grow as a mentor and as a person.

Before we dig in, it's the perfect time to share Marty's story with you. It will help put this section into context.

Marty's life was marked by instability, living with his younger brother, father, and his mother's boyfriend, who was involved in drugs and illegal activities. His mother's neglect and the presence of drugs and guns at home compounded Marty's troubled behavior, leading to multiple arrests and his involvement in a gang.

Despite his challenging circumstances, Marty's mentor, Matt, who was experienced in prison ministries, stepped in to provide much-needed support and guidance. Marty initially seemed responsive, but his journey was marred by setbacks, including further arrests for gun possession and shoplifting. His mentor and others in the community, including his girlfriend's family, rallied around him, providing emotional and practical support, even inviting him into their homes and lives.

Marty experienced moments of transformation that renewed his faith and sense of purpose. However, the temptations and pressures of his past life proved difficult to overcome. Despite the support system in place, Marty struggled to maintain his progress and was ultimately arrested again for violating parole and shoplifting, resulting in a nine-month prison sentence.

Marty's story highlights the harsh reality that not all journeys have a clear or immediate resolution. While his mentors and supporters continue to hope and pray for his eventual success, his path serves as a reminder that change is a long and often difficult process.

Situations like Marty's can leave mentors experiencing a variety of emotions, sparking things like imposter syndrome and leaving them questioning their effectiveness and if they should be part of the program. The information and tools that aim to proactively equip you for any situations that may arise.

2.2 YOUR ROLE AS A MENTOR

As a mentor you are ...

... A FRIEND
Like peer friendships, mentors and mentees support each other both in the good times and in tough times. They teach each other. They help each other. They're honest with each other. And sometimes they have to have hard conversations about concerns they have, asking the right questions at the right time. By being a good listener and engaging in authentic conversations with your mentee, you are helping them develop important life skills.

... A ROLE MODEL
You are expected to set a good example to the mentee for how to live your life. This is not the same as being perfect. Rather, it is about acknowledging your imperfections and sharing your strengths. It is also about advocating for your mentee when dangers to their physical or emotional well-being are present by sharing information that concerns you with the Mentors Care coordinator.

... A CONFIDANT
Building a close relationship with your mentee will help them build better relationships with others in their life as well, such as parents and peers. In the process, your mentee

may tell you things they are not comfortable in sharing with anyone else. Sometimes they may tell you about their hopes, dreams, or insecurities. Other times they may reveal mistakes they have made. Unless your mentee is in trouble and is in need of outside help, it is important to keep these comments private. But, it is understood that you can always share information with the Coordinator in private as your support staff. Your role is to be supportive of your mentee as a person with potential, regardless of the kinds of actions or attitudes they confide in you.

... A NURTURER OF POSSIBILITIES

Your role is to see the gifts and strengths of your mentee and help them flourish personally. You should help your mentee channel their gifts toward actions that make them a resource to others in their family, neighborhood, school, and community.

You are not...

... A MENTOR TO THE FAMILY

Mentors Care asks that you talk to the coordinator before ever contacting a family member. Your role is to provide special attention to your mentee. Your energy and attention are to be focused on providing support to your mentee.

... A SOCIAL WORKER OR DOCTOR

If your mentee tells you about experiences or health conditions that concern you, always turn to the Mentors Care coordinator for help. Although arming yourself with information about, say, a learning disability or abuse may help you understand your mentee better, it is not your responsibility to try and address conditions or situations that require professional help. The coordinator may be able to find additional help for the mentee, including local information and referral services.

... A SAVIOR

You should not see your role in this relationship as coming in to make a young person's life better or to fix their problems. Certainly, your friendship and support can help your mentee overcome hurdles. Your job is to gently guide and direct them in a better way, but ultimately these decisions are up to them. You cannot act as the mentee's parent or guardian in any way, like contacting school faculty or staff. Don't forget that every young person regardless of their circumstances-has gifts and talents that make them more than a "recipient" of your support. You are to empower them to take control of their lives as much as they are able.

2.3 UNDERSTANDING DEFENSE MECHANISMS

Defense mechanisms involve blocking external events from awareness. If some situation is just too much to handle, the person just refuses to experience it. For example, smokers may refuse to admit to themselves that smoking is bad for their health.

Defense mechanisms are psychological strategies that individuals unconsciously employ to protect themselves from anxiety, stress, and internal conflict. These mechanisms often serve as a coping method to deal with uncomfortable emotions or situations, enabling individuals to maintain their mental equilibrium. While they can be helpful in managing immediate emotional distress, over-reliance on defense mechanisms can sometimes hinder personal growth and self-awareness.

Understanding these mechanisms is crucial for mentors, as it allows them to recognize when a mentee is using them and to provide appropriate support and guidance in helping the mentee address underlying issues constructively.

What follows are defense mechanisms that are commonly, and unconsciously used by teens when they are feeling uncomfortable, vulnerable, or exposed.

Regression

The reversion to an earlier stage of development in the face of unacceptable thoughts or impulses. For example, an adolescent who is overwhelmed with fear, anger and growing sexual impulses might become clingy and start exhibiting earlier childhood behaviors he has long since overcome, such as bedwetting. An adult may regress when under a great deal of stress, refusing to leave their bed and engage in normal, everyday activities.

Acting out

Performing an extreme behavior in order to express thoughts or feelings the person feels incapable of otherwise expressing. Instead of saying, "I'm angry with you," a person who acts out may instead throw a book at the person, or punch a hole through a wall. When a person acts out, it can act as a pressure release, and often helps the individual feel calmer and peaceful once again.

Dissociation

When a person loses track of time and instead finds another representation of themselves in order to continue in the moment. A person who dissociates often loses track of time or themselves and their usual thought processes and memories.

Withdrawal

Removing oneself from events and stimuli under the threat of being reminded of painful thoughts & feelings.

Displacement

The redirection of an impulse (usually aggression) onto a powerless substitute target. The target can be a person or an object that can serve as a symbolic substitute. Someone who feels uncomfortable with their sexual desire for a real person may substitute a fetish. Someone who is frustrated by his or her superiors may go home and kick the dog, beat up a family member, or engage in cross-burnings.

Rationalization

The cognitive distortion of "the facts" to make an event or an impulse less threatening. We do it often enough on a fairly conscious level when we provide ourselves with excuses. But for many people, with sensitive egos, making excuses comes so easy that they never are truly aware of it. In other words, many of us are quite prepared to believe our lies.

Reaction formation

The converting of unwanted or dangerous thoughts, feelings or impulses into their opposites. For instance, a woman who is very angry with her boss and would like to quit her job may instead be overly kind and generous toward her boss and express a desire to keep working there forever. She is incapable of expressing the negative emotions of anger and unhappiness with her job, and instead becomes overly kind to publicly demonstrate her lack of anger and unhappiness.

Compartmentalization

A lesser form of dissociation, wherein parts of oneself are separated from awareness of other parts and behaving as if one had separate sets of values. An example might be an honest person who cheats on their income tax return and keeps their two value systems distinct and un-integrated while remaining unconscious of the cognitive dissonance.

Undoing

The attempt to take back an unconscious behavior or thought that is unacceptable or hurtful. For instance, after realizing you just insulted your significant other unintentionally, you might spend the next hour praising their beauty, charm and intellect. By "undoing" the previous action, the person is attempting to counteract the damage done by the original comment, hoping the two will balance one another out.

2.4 BOUNDARY SETTING

Boundary setting is a crucial process of establishing clear and healthy limits in relationships to protect one's emotional, physical, and mental well-being. By defining what is acceptable and unacceptable behavior, boundaries help maintain respect, reduce stress, and prevent burnout. For mentors, setting boundaries is essential to maintain a professional and effective relationship with their mentees. It ensures that both parties understand their roles and responsibilities, fostering a supportive and safe environment for personal growth. Understanding and implementing boundary setting can lead to more productive and balanced interactions, allowing mentors to provide the best possible guidance while preserving their own well-being.

It's important to set personal boundaries to maintain a healthy mentor-mentee relationship.

1. Initial Conversation
    - Discuss boundaries during the first meeting.
    - Explain the importance of boundaries for both parties.

2. Define Specific Limits
   - Clearly outline what is acceptable and what's not.
   - Use concrete examples to illustrate boundaries.
3. Regular Check-ins
   - Periodically review and adjust boundaries, as needed.
   - Encourage open communication about how the mentoring relationship is going.
4. Model Boundaries
   - Demonstrate good boundary-setting through your behavior.
   - Respect the mentee's boundaries to set an example.
5. Seek Support
   - If boundaries are challenged, seek advice from the program coordinator.

Responding to Boundary Challenges

- Stay Calm. Address the issue without anger or frustration.
- Reiterate boundaries by reminding the mentee of the agreed-upon limits.

- If a boundary isn't working, discuss and modify it. If it's repeatedly crossed, involve your program coordinator.

Sample Boundary Statements

- "I'm happy to help you during our scheduled meetings, but I'm not available for calls or texts outside those times."

- "I care about your well-being, but I'm not equipped to provide the support you need for this issue. Let's find a professional who can help."

- "I prefer to keep our conversations focused on your goals and challenges. I'll share personal experiences when relevant, but I want to keep the focus on you."

By setting clear, consistent, and respectful boundaries, mentors can create a supportive and sustainable mentoring relationship that benefits both them and their mentees.

2.5 FIVE STEP REFLECTION ON ROUGH VISITS

Following the steps outlined below will help you process and reflect upon the emotions of a visit with your student that was particularly challenging – taking care of yourself now while also preparing for the next time you and your mentee are together.

Step 1. Reflect and Recognize

- Take a moment to reflect on the visit.
    - What specific events or interactions made this visit challenging?
    - How did I feel during and after the visit?
    - What thoughts or reactions did I have in response to the mentee's behavior?

Step 2. Vent and Validate

- Allow yourself to express your feelings.
    - What emotions am I experiencing right now (e.g., frustration, disappointment, sadness)?
    - How can I express these feelings in a healthy way (e.g., talking to someone, writing them down)?
    - What do I need to feel supported and heard in this moment?

Step 3. Analyze and Learn

- Evaluate the situation objectively.
    - What might have triggered the mentee's behavior or reactions?
    - Were there any external factors (e.g., school stress, family issues) that could have influenced the visit?
    - What part of my approach could I improve or change for next time?
    - What can I learn from this experience to apply in future visits?

Step 4. Plan and Prepare

- Develop a strategy for future visits.
    - What specific goals do I want to set for the next visit?
    - What strategies or techniques can I use to address the issues that arose?
    - How can I better support my mentee in managing their challenges?
    - What resources or tools might help me in preparing for the next visit?

Step 5. Self-Care and Recharge

- Engage in activities that replenish your energy and well-being.
    - What activities help me relax and rejuvenate (e.g., exercise, hobbies, spending time with loved ones)?
    - How can I ensure I get adequate rest and relaxation before the next visit?
    - What self-care practices can I incorporate into my routine to maintain my well-being?
    - Who can I reach out to for support or guidance if I need it?

2.6 PROCESSING FEELINGS OF REJECTION

Assessing the situation

- What exactly happened that made me feel rejected?
- Are there specific actions or words from the mentee that triggered these feelings?
- How intense are my feelings right now, and what are they (e.g., sadness, frustration, disappointment)?
- How can I remind myself that rejection is often not personal but rather a reflection of the mentee's own struggles?
- What can I do to be kind to myself in this moment?
- What would I say to a friend or colleague who is going through a similar situation?
- How can I acknowledge my efforts and dedication as a mentor, regardless of the mentee's response?

Moving Forward

- What are some positive aspects of my mentoring relationship that I can focus on?
- How can I learn from this experience to improve my approach in the future?

- What are some practical steps I can take to rebuild trust and rapport with my mentee?
- What activities help me relax and feel better that I can engage in right now?
- Who can I talk to about my feelings for support and perspective?

How can I ensure that I maintain a healthy balance between my mentoring role and personal well-being?

2.7 TWELVE STAGES OF BURNOUT

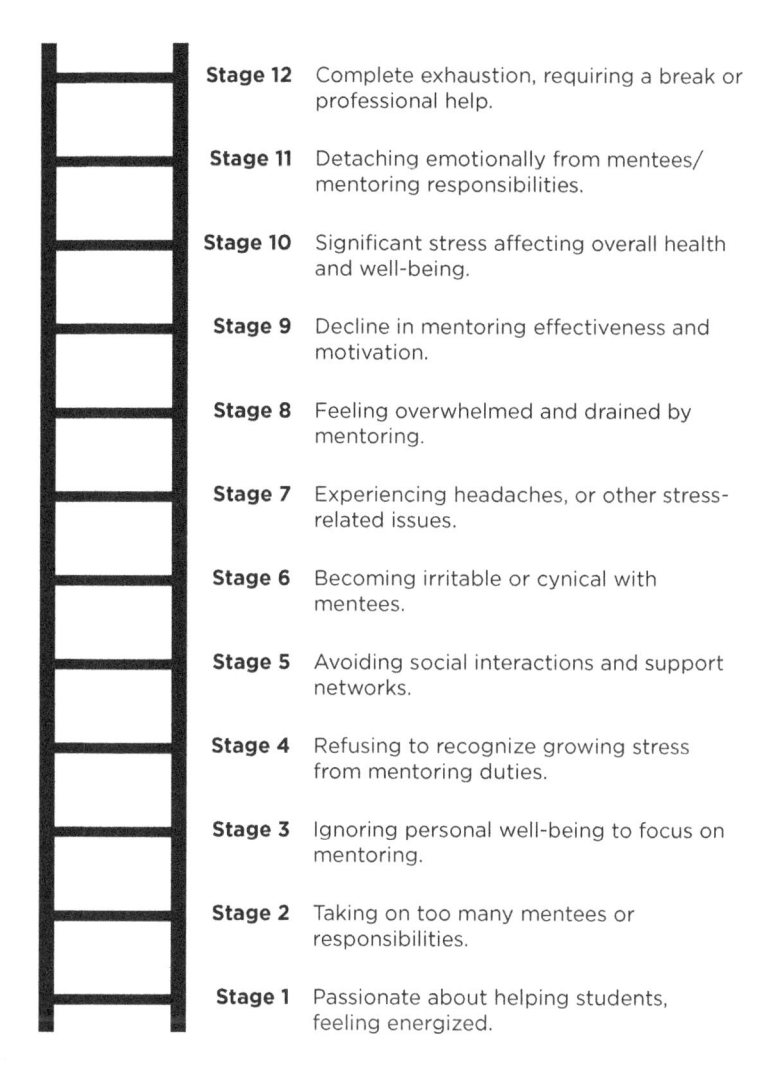

Stage 12 Complete exhaustion, requiring a break or professional help.

Stage 11 Detaching emotionally from mentees/mentoring responsibilities.

Stage 10 Significant stress affecting overall health and well-being.

Stage 9 Decline in mentoring effectiveness and motivation.

Stage 8 Feeling overwhelmed and drained by mentoring.

Stage 7 Experiencing headaches, or other stress-related issues.

Stage 6 Becoming irritable or cynical with mentees.

Stage 5 Avoiding social interactions and support networks.

Stage 4 Refusing to recognize growing stress from mentoring duties.

Stage 3 Ignoring personal well-being to focus on mentoring.

Stage 2 Taking on too many mentees or responsibilities.

Stage 1 Passionate about helping students, feeling energized.

If you are experiencing burnout beyond stage 7 please let your Mentors Care Coordinator know so that they can offer support and self care options.

2.8 FIVE TYPES OF IMPOSTER SYNDROME

The superhero says, "If I were really competent, I would be able to do it all and do it easily and well."

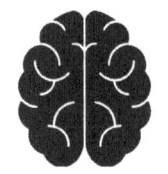

The genius says, "I should do this quickly and easily. If I can't, I'm not smart.

The expert says, "I should already know this and shouldn't need to hear it more than once."

The perfectionist says, "I should always be perfect. My work should always get an A+."

The soloist says, "I must do everything myself otherwise maybe I didn't contribute."

Do you recognize any of these in yourself or your mentee?

When these thoughts creep up for either of you, write down three things that you know that you are really good at and don't let the imposter take over!

2.9 SUCCESS STORIES TO FUEL YOU

Allison's Story

Allison first came to our attention through the high school counseling department. Her mom had suffered a stroke and was living in a nursing home. They lost their home, and Allison was staying with her boyfriend. She was also dealing with stress-induced seizures. When we first met Allison, it was clear how upset she was, and it was noted that she might become homeless if her boyfriend kicked her out. Soon enough, he did, and Allison moved in with a concerned adult who had heard her story.

Through a referral initiated by her mentor, a church friend offered to take Allison in, and despite her fears, Allison moved in with them. Allison was challenging to handle, often angry and sensitive, but understanding her difficult past made her behavior more understandable. Her father was an alcoholic who left when she was 13, and her mother's erratic behavior and eventual stroke, due to meth use, forced Allison into a caretaker role for her younger sister.

Despite her struggles, Allison never missed school. When her mom's condition worsened, it was insisted that Allison visit her in the hospital. Watching her care for her mom was heartbreaking. As her mom's condition deteriorated, Allison had to face tough medical decisions. Ultimately, she decided on hospice care for her mom.

Allison showed incredible strength, continuing school while visiting her mom daily. She made the difficult decision to stop life-prolonging measures, and she was there when her mom passed away. Her mom's death was a quiet, sad affair, revealing the devastating impact of drugs on their lives.

Despite everything, Allison graduated. With some encouragement, she reconnected with her dad. With his help, she got a job, an apartment, and a car, and planned to attend community college.

Nicole's Story

Nicole didn't initially stand out as needing urgent help, but her poor attendance and grades put her on the at-risk list. Her mentor struggled to engage her, as she was very guarded and sad.

The breakthrough came when Nicole revealed her mother's regular physical and emotional abuse. Despite reporting this to CPS, no action was taken. At 18, Nicole's mother forced her out, but she moved in with her grandfather, providing some stability despite the poor living conditions. Living with her grandfather, Nicole's attendance and grades improved. She explained that frequent moves to avoid eviction had previously disrupted her education.

Nicole faced a major setback when her boyfriend broke up with her, leaving her devastated. She also suffered from severe abdominal pain but had no means to see a doctor. A group of generous doctors provided free medical care, diagnosing her with treatable STDs, which added to her emotional distress when she learned her ex-boyfriend had lied about his past. With medical treatment and her mentor's support, Nicole recovered both physically and emotionally. She persevered, ultimately graduating with a high school diploma.

Nicole found a nursing school offering financial aid, allowing her to pursue a new career. She occasionally visits to share her progress, showing resilience and a bright future ahead.

Julia's Story

Julia was brought to our attention by another student who overheard her talking about her troubling behavior. When we first met, Julia's language and attitude were shocking, but she began to open up about her difficult life. Julia didn't know her mother well, lived with her dad and two younger brothers, and had essentially become the caretaker of the household. Her relationship with her father was strained, and her middle school years were marked by trouble, including drug possession and fighting.

Julia's mentor, experienced with troubled teens, faced initial resistance but began to break through her walls. One significant moment was when Julia had an emotional outburst after fighting with her boyfriend. The mentor managed to calm her down, establishing a bond of trust.

Over time, Julia's school performance and attitude improved. She went from D's and F's to A's and B's, realizing she was smart and could excel in school. Her language also improved, and she began to show gratitude and respect.

Julia graduated with good grades and a plan to become a nurse. She now smiles often, uses polite language, and expresses gratitude regularly. The transformation in Julia has been remarkable, showing the profound impact of mentorship and support.

Trent's Story

Trent was first introduced through a high school staff member who noticed he was struggling and could benefit from a mentor. Despite his difficult past, Trent was open about his life without seeking pity. He had made mistakes at a young age, which his family never forgave, leading to his homelessness. During a court appearance, Trent's mentor witnessed his mother's cold and cruel demeanor, explaining why Trent ended up homeless.

One summer night, feeling utterly hopeless, Trent attempted to end his life by riding his bike into oncoming traffic. Miraculously, he survived and sought refuge in a church, where a family took him in. This stability allowed Trent to return to school with hope of graduating.

Trent and his mentor worked together to address his immediate needs, set future goals, and plan for life after graduation. Trent's past failures haunted him, affecting his grades. However, his mentor played a pivotal role in boosting his self-worth, encouraging him to work hard. Trent spent many hours after school in the library, eventually improving his grades and passing all his classes.

Conversations about college initially seemed out of reach for Trent, but he took a chance and applied to a small local college, receiving grants and scholarships. Trent enrolled with Mentors Care helping with initial college expenses and supplies.

Tyler's Story

Tyler first caught our attention sitting alone in the public library, looking unkempt and sad. The librarians mentioned he often sat by himself. When approached and invited to the office, Tyler agreed, looking surprised but cooperative.

In the office, it became clear Tyler was struggling, missing school frequently and having all D's and F's. When asked how he was doing, Tyler broke down in tears, admitting he was very lonely. This struck an emotional chord, and Tyler was quickly paired with a mentor who became a supportive friend and cheerleader.

Tyler's mentor noticed he never made eye contact and had a nervous tic, but despite his shyness, Tyler quickly engaged with the mentoring process. His mentor challenged him to improve his attendance, promising to be there every week if

Tyler did not miss school. Tyler's attendance improved dramatically, and with it, his grades.

Though Tyler still kept to himself, his mentor encouraged him to explore extracurricular activities. Tyler expressed an interest in art but lamented the lack of an art club. His mentor then challenged him to start one, with the promise of a field trip to see a mural being painted by a well-known artist.

Tyler took on the challenge, organized the club, recruited a teacher sponsor, and received approval from the principal. The club began small but grew steadily, eventually holding two meetings a week.

The transformation in Tyler was profound. He became more confident, lifting his head and engaging with others. One morning, he greeted his mentor with a smile, surrounded by his art club friends, chatting and laughing. This moment marked a significant milestone in Tyler's journey from loneliness to finding his place and passion in school.

PART THREE

Resources, Tools, & Activities to Support Your Mentees

About This Section

Building trusting relationships takes work. Showing up consistently is a starting point. The tools in this section supplement your Talking Points® to help you get to know your mentee – and them to know you – on a deeper level.

3.1 ABOUT THE TALKING POINTS®

Let's talk about why your Talking Points® are so valuable.

Over the years, there have been many mentors that have said they didn't need the Talking Points® because talking with teenagers is easy. This may be true for some but inevitably, a large number of mentors will get "stuck" talking about the same topics each week – students will want to talk about the girlfriend or boyfriend every week.

Of course, this is important to a teenager, and yes you will have those conversations. But there is so much lost opportunity to help this student grow and learn valuable life lessons if the same topics are discussed over and over.

The Talking Points® are designed to help the student first understand the importance of an education, moving into what it takes to be a successful person to then what do you see in your future.

The Talking Points® are a valuable tool to help you both grow in your relationship of trust and friendship while taking a moment to understand themselves and the world around them.

Take a moment before the meeting and glean over the Talking Points® and leading questions before your meeting. It is not about reading the information verbatim, it is about using it as a valuable tool to guide you both into a meaningful conversation.

3.2 THE CARE MODEL

The CARE Model is a comprehensive approach designed to help you build strong, trusting, and meaningful relationships with your students. As a mentor, your role is pivotal in guiding, supporting, and inspiring the next generation. The CARE Model provides you with a framework to establish a solid foundation of trust and rapport, which are essential for a successful mentoring relationship.

What is the CARE Model?

The CARE Model stands for Consistency, Active Listening, Respect, and Empathy. These four pillars are the cornerstones of effective mentoring. By embracing and implementing these principles, you can create a safe and supportive environment where your students feel valued, understood, and motivated to grow.

Purpose of the CARE Model:

- **CONSISTENCY:** To build reliability and dependability in your interactions, ensuring that your student feels secure and supported.

- **ACTIVE LISTENING:** To show genuine interest and understanding of your student's thoughts and feelings, fostering open and honest communication.

- **RESPECT:** To honor and value your student's perspectives, experiences, and boundaries, creating a space where they feel respected and appreciated.

- **EMPATHY:** To connect on a deeper emotional level by understanding and sharing your student's feelings, demonstrating that you truly care about their well-being.

By following the CARE Model, you will not only enhance your mentoring skills but also create a nurturing environment that empowers your student to overcome challenges, build confidence, and achieve their goals. This model is designed to be a practical and effective guide to help you navigate the complexities of the mentoring relationship with compassion and professionalism.

C-Consistency

Be dependable and consistent in your interactions. Regular and predictable meetings create a stable environment that fosters trust.

Always show up on time, keep your commitments, and be here when you say you will be. Consistency helps build a reliable foundation for your relationship.

A - Active Listening

Show genuine interest in what the student says by listening attentively. Active listening involves fully concentrating, understanding, responding, and remembering what the students share.

Use open-ended questions, paraphrase what the student says to show understanding, and provide feedback that acknowledges their feelings and thoughts. Avoid interrupting and give them your full attention.

R - Respect

Demonstrate respect for the student's feelings, experiences, and perspectives. Treat them with kindness and consideration.

Acknowledge their opinions, be mindful of their boundaries, and show appreciation for their efforts and achievements. Respect their privacy and keep sensitive information confidential.

E - Empathy

Show empathy by understanding and sharing the feelings of the student. Empathy helps in building a deeper connection and shows that you genuinely care about their well-being.

Validate their emotions, express understanding and concern, and offer support without judgment. Use phrases like "I can see why you feel that way" or "It sounds like that was really tough for you."

3.3 SHOWING UP FOR YOUR STUDENT

Have you ever been stood up by someone for a meeting?
How about for a date?
How about for something as simple as lunch?
How did that make you feel?

You probably felt emotions like embarrassment, anger, hurt, or simply feeling not valued by the person who didn't show up for you.

Now add to those same feelings the difficulties of being a teen, and dealing with the struggles of school stress, self-esteem issues, a difficult home life, homework, anxiety, depression, and all of the other things that adolescents have to endure. Adults not being dependable for teens only amplify their struggles, leaving them alone and feeling angry, hurt, or even embarrassed.

The majority of our students come from home lives that are probably much different than the home that you grew up in. Many of them come from dysfunctional families where fighting, substance abuse, financial issues, and even mental illness are the norm. Their parents, oftentimes, let them down.

A large percentage of Mentors Care kids are accustomed to broken promises and unfulfilled commitments from adults. This is why it is so critical that you show up weekly once you have committed to being a mentor.

Of course, things happen that cause you to miss your mentoring meetings at times. Cars break down, work schedules interfere, and mentors get sick just like everyone else. We Understand that!

Once you establish a bond with your student (which doesn't usually take long), they will look forward to and get excited about your visits to mentor them. They are disappointed when their meetings with you are canceled.

Sometimes the kids take it personally and think that you don't like them or don't enjoy visiting with them.

There is nothing worse than a student peeking around the door and asking if their mentor is coming and not being able to answer. It happens, and it is devastating. Honestly, it would be better to not have had a mentor at all, then a mentor that just doesn't show up without a reason why.

Communication is key. Let us know if we can reschedule, we can communicate this to the student.

One of the key Talking Points® in our curriculum is titled, "Why Showing Up Is Half the Battle." This rings true for our kids - showing up to school really is critical. Showing up is just as important for adults, as we must be the example of what we hope our kids will become.

We encourage you to be consistent in showing up weekly for your student. It really does make all the difference. By just showing up each week for your student, you will earn their trust, build relationships, and demonstrate to them just how committed you are to them!

3.4 FIVE CONVERSATION TYPES FOR MENTORS

Introductory Conversations

Introduce the mentee to the mentoring process, setting clear expectations and goals. Establish communication norms and provide information on available resources.

Getting to Know You Conversations

Build rapport by discussing the mentee's background, interests, and aspirations. Use open-ended questions to encourage sharing and understanding.

Maintaining the Relationship

Sustain the mentoring relationship through regular check-ins, feedback, and support. Celebrate successes and adapt to the mentee's evolving needs.

Exit Conversations

Conclude the mentoring relationship by reflecting on achievements and future steps. Provide and receive feedback to ensure a positive closure.

Difficult Conversations

Address and resolve conflicts or sensitive issues with empathy and problem-solving. Focus on the issue at hand and aim for a constructive resolution.

3.5 FEELINGS WHEEL (ABBREVIATED VERSION)

```
        Depressed    Anxious
   Pain                    Vulnerable

Grief    Sadness      Fear         Insecure
         (Loss)   (Feeling
                  judgement)

Astonished  Surprised    Joy        Happy
            (Caught    (Gain)
            off guard)

   Overwhelmed            Excited
        Startled    Grateful
```

This is a simplified version of a common tool used to help understand and identify feelings. A more detailed version is available in your digital resources-to-go as well as your coordinators office.

3.6 CONVERSATION TOOLS FOR COMMON TEEN ISSUES

We want to acknowledge that this list is *far* from inclusive. As we've mentioned in other areas of this guide, issues change over time but we've included these as a baseline of issues that commonly show up to provide general guidance in navigating these situations.

In all cases, refer to your coordinator if you have concerns and/or think your student may need professional counseling, therapy, or support beyond the mentoring experience.

We can't stress this enough: If in doubt, ask your coordinator for direction.

Depression

Persistent feelings of sadness, hopelessness, and a lack of interest or pleasure in activities.

You may recognize signs such as withdrawal from friends and activities, changes in appetite or sleep patterns, and expressions of worthlessness.

AVOID SAYING THINGS LIKE:
- "Just cheer up."
- "It's all in your head."
- "Other people have it worse."

- "Snap out of it."
- "You should be grateful for what you have."

TOOLS TO HELP:
- **Active Listening:** Show empathy and understanding by listening without judgment.
- **Encouragement:** Encourage positive activities that the teen enjoys or once enjoyed.
- **Consistent Support:** Check in regularly to show you care and are there for them.

Anxiety

Excessive worry, nervousness, or fear about everyday situations.

Look for signs like restlessness, difficulty concentrating, rapid heartbeat, and avoidance of certain situations. Encourage relaxation techniques and provide reassurance.

AVOID SAYING:
- "Calm down."
- "You're overreacting."
- "Just relax, there's nothing to worry about."
- "Stop being so anxious."
- "It's not a big deal."

TOOLS TO HELP:

- **Breathing Exercises:** Teach simple breathing exercises to help manage anxiety.
- **Mindfulness:** Introduce mindfulness techniques to help teens stay grounded.
- **Validation:** Acknowledge their feelings and reassure them that it's okay to feel anxious.
- **Problem-Solving**: Help them break down their worries into manageable parts.

Grief

Deep sorrow, especially caused by someone's death, but also due to other significant losses such as the end of a friendship or parental divorce.

Be supportive and patient, allowing teens to express their feelings and providing comfort. Grief is a profound and complex emotion that requires deep understanding and care. While it's important to recognize when a mentee is experiencing grief, it is not our role to guide them through this process. Instead, we create a space for them to feel seen and heard. If you sense your mentee is struggling with grief, please notify your coordinator so they can ensure the right support is provided.

AVOID SAYING:

- "They're in a better place."

- "I know how you feel."
- "At least they lived a long life."
- "You need to move on."
- "Everything happens for a reason."

TOOLS TO HELP:
- **Listening:** Provide a safe space for them to express their feelings without interruption.
- **Empathy:** Show empathy and understanding, acknowledging their pain.
- **Rituals:** Encourage healthy rituals to honor their loss, such as writing a letter or creating a memory book.

Self-Harm

Deliberate infliction of harm to one's body as a way to cope with emotional pain.

Signs include unexplained cuts, bruises, or burns, and wearing long sleeves even in hot weather. It's important to address this behavior with sensitivity and connect the teen with mental health professionals (via your coordinator)

AVOID SAYING:
- "Why would you do that to yourself?"
- "That's just for attention."

- "Stop hurting yourself."
- "You need to get over it."
- "You're being dramatic."

TOOLS TO HELP:
- **Non-Judgmental Support:** Approach the topic calmly and without judgment.
- **Expressive Activities:** Suggest expressive activities like drawing, writing, or music as alternatives to self-harm.

Eating Disorders

Unhealthy eating behaviors, which may include extreme dieting, overeating, or preoccupation with food, body shape, and weight.

There may be noticeable weight loss or gain, obsession with food or calories, and frequent comments about being fat. Encouraging a positive body image and seeking specialized help is important.

AVOID SAYING:
- "Just eat more/less."
- "You don't look sick."
- "It's just a phase."
- "You're being selfish."

- "Stop being so obsessed with food."

TOOLS TO HELP:
- **Encouragement:** Encourage healthy eating habits without focusing on weight.
- **Body Positivity:** Promote a positive body image and self-esteem.

Substance Abuse

The use of drugs or alcohol in a way that is harmful or risky.

Be aware of changes in behavior, declining academic performance, and secretive actions. Have open conversations about the risks.

<u>Important note: If your student looks to be under the influence while meeting with them, you must notify your Mentors Care Coordinator.</u>

AVOID SAYING:
- "Just say no."
- "You should know better."
- "You're ruining your life."
- "Why can't you just stop?"
- "You're making a big mistake."

TOOLS TO HELP:

- **Open Dialogue:** Have open and honest conversations about the dangers of substance abuse.

- **Healthy Alternatives:** Help them find healthy alternatives to cope with stress and peer pressure.

Bullying/Cyberbullying

Repeated aggressive behavior intended to hurt another person, physically or emotionally, which can also occur online.

Be aware of things like unexplained injuries, lost or destroyed belongings, frequent headaches or stomach aches, and changes in eating habits. Offer support and guide them towards appropriate interventions.

AVOID SAYING:

- "Just ignore it."

- "Fight back."

- "It's just part of growing up."

- "Don't be a tattletale."

- "You're too sensitive."

TOOLS TO HELP:

- **Supportive Listening:** Listen to their experiences without dismissing their feelings.

- **Empowerment**: Empower them by building their self-confidence and teaching assertiveness.

- **Digital Safety:** Educate them on online safety and how to block/report cyberbullies. (Refer to 2nd year Talking Points® – #7)

Trauma

Emotional response to a distressing event such as abuse, violence, or witnessing a traumatic incident.

Symptoms might include flashbacks, nightmares, and severe anxiety. Create a safe environment for the teen to talk about their experience.

AVOID SAYING:
- "Just get over it."
- "It could have been worse."
- "You're safe now, so forget about it."
- "Why can't you move on?"
- "Stop dwelling on the past."

TOOLS TO HELP:
- **Validation:** Acknowledge their trauma and validate their feelings.
- **Safety and Trust:** Create a safe and trusting environment for them to open up.

3.7 ENGAGEMENT/RELATIONSHIP BUILDING ACTIVITIES & GAMES

Mentors Care Uno®

SETUP

Shuffle the Uno cards and deal 7 cards to each player. Place the remaining deck face down in the center as the draw pile. Turn over the top card to create a discard pile.

GAMEPLAY

Play Uno as you normally would, but with a twist. In addition to the regular Uno rules, each card color corresponds to a different type of personal question. Here's a breakdown:

- Red Cards: Share a memorable childhood experience.
- Blue Cards: Tell me something you wish you could change.
- Green Cards: Describe a hobby or interest you're passionate about.
- Yellow Cards: Share a funny or embarrassing moment from your life.

SPECIAL CARDS

You can incorporate special Uno cards to add more interaction:

- Skip Card: The Student can choose to skip the question.

- Reverse Card: Change the direction of play and ask the mentor.

- Wild Card: The player who plays a Wild Card gets to choose any color and ask a question related to that color.

- Draw Two Card: The player who receives the Draw Two card answers two questions of the same color.

Would You Rather...

Use these questions as conversation starters to engage with your students and learn more about them. Don't forget to share your preferences with them as well!

FOOD EDITION

1. Would you rather eat pizza or pasta for the rest of your life?
2. Would you rather only eat sweet foods or only eat savory foods?
3. Would you rather have a permanent taste of garlic in your mouth or onions in your mouth?
4. Would you rather eat ice cream in winter or hot soup in summer?
5. Would you rather only eat breakfast foods or only eat dessert foods?
6. Would you rather never be able to eat chocolate again or never be able to eat cheese again?
7. Would you rather eat only raw vegetables or only cooked vegetables?
8. Would you rather have a personal chef or a personal nutritionist?
9. Would you rather drink only water or only soda for the rest of your life?

10. Would you rather give up your favorite food forever or be allowed to eat only your favorite food forever?

VACATION EDITION

1. Would you rather travel to the mountains or the beach for a vacation?
2. Would you rather take a luxury cruise or a budget backpacking trip?
3. Would you rather explore a new city every day or relax in one resort for a week?
4. Would you rather have an adventure vacation with activities like hiking and rafting or a relaxation vacation with spa treatments?
5. Would you rather visit historical sites or theme parks?
6. Would you rather go on a safari in Africa or a tour of European capitals?
7. Would you rather travel alone or with a group of friends?
8. Would you rather go on a road trip across the country or a flight to a foreign country?
9. Would you rather have unlimited funds for a vacation but no time off work or plenty of time off but a limited budget for a vacation?
10. Would you rather travel to a tropical island or a snowy ski resort?

SCHOOL EDITION

1. Would you rather have a test every week but no homework or a big project every month and regular homework?
2. Would you rather be the smartest kid in school or the most popular?
3. Would you rather learn a new language fluently in a year or master a new musical instrument in a year?
4. Would you rather have a longer summer vacation or more breaks throughout the school year?
5. Would you rather have classes start later in the day or have shorter school days?
6. Would you rather do all your schoolwork on a computer or with traditional paper and pencil?
7. Would you rather go to a school with no sports teams or no arts programs?
8. Would you rather have a teacher who is funny and engaging but gives a lot of homework or a teacher who is boring but gives little homework?
9. Would you rather have a school dress code or a uniform?
10. Would you rather go on a school field trip to a museum or an amusement park?

ENTERTAINMENT EDITION

1. Would you rather watch movies or TV shows for the rest of your life?
2. Would you rather listen to only one genre of music forever or never listen to music again?
3. Would you rather have free tickets to any concert or free tickets to any sports game?
4. Would you rather be a famous actor or a famous musician?
5. Would you rather play video games all day or watch movies all day?
6. Would you rather be a contestant on a game show or a reality TV show?
7. Would you rather read books or watch movies?
8. Would you rather see your favorite band perform live or meet your favorite actor in person?
9. Would you rather have an unlimited Netflix subscription or an unlimited Spotify subscription?
10. Would you rather be the star of a popular TV show or the author of a bestselling book?

FUTURE EDITION

1. Would you rather live in a big city or a small town?
2. Would you rather have a job you love with a low salary or a job you dislike with a high salary?
3. Would you rather be famous for your talent or for your intelligence?
4. Would you rather have the ability to see into the future or change the past?
5. Would you rather be able to fly or become invisible?
6. Would you rather own your own business or be the CEO of a large corporation?
7. Would you rather travel to space or explore the deepest parts of the ocean?
8. Would you rather be able to speak every language in the world or play every musical instrument?
9. Would you rather always know the right answer or always make the right decision?
10. Would you rather have a dream home in the countryside or a luxury apartment in the city?

Desert Island Game

SCENARIO OVERVIEW:

Imagine that you and your mentor are stranded on a deserted island after a shipwreck. The island is lush and beautiful, but also wild and uninhabited. You have to survive using the resources available on the island and the items you managed to salvage from the ship. This is a chance to get creative and share your thoughts and preferences.

INITIAL CHOICES:

Question: "You can choose three items from the shipwreck to bring with you to the island. What would they be and why?"

Follow-up: Discuss the reasons behind their choices, focusing on practicality, emotional comfort, or survival needs.

SHELTER:

Question: "How would you go about building a shelter on the island? What materials would you use?"

Follow-up: Talk about the student's approach to problem-solving and their creative thinking.

FOOD AND WATER:

Question: "What strategies would you use to find food and water on the island?"

Follow-up: Discuss their knowledge about nature, survival skills, and resourcefulness.

ENTERTAINMENT AND HOBBIES:

Question: "With no modern technology, how would you entertain yourself on the island? What hobbies or activities would you engage in?"

Follow-up: Explore the student's interests, hobbies, and how they like to spend their free time.

COMMUNICATION AND RESCUE:

Question: "If you could send a message in a bottle or create a signal for rescue, what would it say or look like?"

Follow-up: Discuss their thoughts on communication, creativity, and how they would prioritize what to convey.

COMPANIONSHIP:

Question: "If you could have one person (real or fictional) with you on the island, who would it be and why?"

Follow-up: Talk about their relationships, role models, and what qualities they value in others.

REFLECTION:

Question: "What do you think you would learn about yourself if you were really in this situation? How do you think you would change?"

Follow-up: Encourage self-reflection and discuss potential personal growth, resilience, and adaptability.

Shopping Spree Game

HOW TO USE THIS SCENARIO

Set the Stage. Explain the scenario to the student, emphasizing the need to choose wisely and budget their money.

Ask Open-Ended Questions. Use the outlined questions to guide the conversation, encouraging detailed answers and thoughtful consideration.

Listen Actively. Show genuine interest in the student's responses, ask follow-up questions, and relate their answers to real-life budgeting and decision-making scenarios.

Share Your Own Choices. As a mentor, share your own hypothetical choices to model openness and encourage a two-way conversation.

Reflect Together. At the end of the discussion, reflect on what you both learned about each other through this exercise and discuss any insights gained.

SCENARIO OVERVIEW:
"Imagine you've just received a gift of $500 to spend on anything you want. However, there's a catch: you can only spend this money in one store of your choice. Think carefully about where you'd go and what you'd buy because once you pick a store, you can't change your mind!"

Question: "With your $500, which store would you choose to shop at and why?"

Follow-up: Discuss the reasons behind their choice, such as favorite brands, product variety, or specific items they've been wanting.

Question: "What are the top three items you would buy in that store? Why are these items important to you?"

Follow-up: Explore their priorities and what they value most (e.g., entertainment, practicality, hobbies).

Question: "How would you allocate your $500 among the items you want? Can you break down the costs for me?"
Follow-up: Discuss their budgeting skills and whether they consider getting the most value for their money or splurging on a few high-cost items.

Question: "If you find out that your top three items exceed $500, how would you adjust your choices? What would you sacrifice or change?"

Follow-up: Talk about decision-making and the ability to compromise or prioritize.

Question: "Do you think your choices reflect things you need or things you want? Why?"

Follow-up: Discuss the difference between needs and wants and how they made their decisions.

Question: "If the store also offered experiences (like classes, trips, or events), would you spend your money differently? How?"

Follow-up: Explore whether they value experiences over material items and why.

Question: "Which of your chosen items do you think will make you happiest in the long run? Why?"

Follow-up: Discuss the concept of long-term satisfaction versus immediate gratification.

Timeline of Me

1. Birth date and place of birth
2. Earliest memory you can recall
3. First day of kindergarten or first grade
4. A memorable event or achievement during elementary school
5. First significant family trip or vacation
6. The summer you consider the best and why
7. The release date of a movie that became your favorite
8. When you discovered a hobby you love and what it is
9. When and how you met your best friend
10. When you got your first pet and what kind of pet it was
11. When you moved to a new house or city for the first time
12. First day of junior high or middle school
13. An academic achievement or award you're proud of
14. The first time you joined a school club or sports team
15. The first job or chore you did for money
16. A major family event, like a wedding, reunion, or a new sibling
17. When you read a book that became your favorite

18. The date when you learned a significant new skill (e.g., riding a bike, cooking)
19. A challenging event or period and how you overcame it
20. First day of high school
21. When you made a new significant friend during high school
22. A school project or presentation that was significant to you
23. The first trip you took without your family Important
24. Any personal achievement you are particularly proud of
25. The date when you got your driver's license
26. Your favorite event in high school, like a dance, sports game, or concert
27. When you started your first romantic relationship

Open Ended Questions

1. What are some of your favorite hobbies or activities, and why do you enjoy them?
2. Can you tell me about a recent accomplishment that you're proud of?
3. What are some goals you have for the next few years, and how do you plan to achieve them?
4. Who is someone you admire, and what qualities do you like about them?
5. Can you describe a time when you faced a challenge and how you dealt with it?
6. What are some things that make you feel happy and fulfilled?
7. If you could change one thing about your school, what would it be and why?
8. What is a subject or topic you're really passionate about, and what sparked your interest in it?
9. How do you like to spend your free time, and why do those activities appeal to you?
10. What are some ways you like to relax or de-stress when things get overwhelming?
11. What kind of career do you see yourself pursuing, and what attracts you to that field?

12. If you could travel anywhere in the world, where would you go and what would you do there?

13. What are some things you hope to achieve in your life, both personally and professionally?

14. How do you imagine your life will be in ten years?

15. What skills or talents do you have that you think could help you in the future?

16. What is your favorite subject in school, and what do you like about it?

17. Can you describe a teacher who has had a significant impact on you, and how they influenced you?

18. What do you find most challenging about school, and how do you manage those challenges?

19. How do you prefer to study or learn new things?

20. What are some projects or assignments that you found particularly interesting or rewarding?

21. Who are the people you feel closest to, and what makes those relationships special?

22. How do you handle conflicts or disagreements with friends or family?

23. What qualities do you look for in a friend, and why are those important to you?

24. Can you share an experience where you helped someone or made a positive difference in someone's life?

25. How do you feel about social media, and how does it impact your relationships?
26. What are some personal values or principles that are important to you?
27. How do you stay motivated when you're working towards a difficult goal?
28. Can you describe a time when you learned something important about yourself?
29. What are some areas of your life where you would like to grow or improve?
30. How do you cope with stress or difficult emotions?
31. What books, movies, or TV shows have had a big impact on you, and why?
32. Do you have any creative outlets, like writing, art, or music?
33. Can you tell me about them?
34. What causes or issues are you passionate about, and how do you get involved in them?
35. How do you stay informed about the world around you?
36. What are some activities or projects you would love to try if you had the chance?

RESOURCES QUICK REFERENCE GRID

Situation	Response	Resource
"What if my mentee doesn't open up to me?"	Building trust takes time. Be patient, show genuine interest, and create a safe space for open communication.	**Ice Breaker Questions** (see page 76)
"I'm worried I won't have all the answers to my mentee's questions."	We don't want not to have all the answers. Your role is to guide and support, you can always help find resources or learn together.	**Relationship Building Activities** (see page 62)
"I'm concerned about handling difficult or sensitive topics with my mentee."	Difficult conversations are sure to arise. We have provided resources to help guide you through them.	**Difficult Conversations** (see page 52)
"My mentee is always fighting against me and acting out."	Stay patient and consistent. Most of the mentees find it hard to trust people and use defense mechanisms to keep them from getting close.	**Defense Mechanisms** (see page 23)
"I need to be clear about when and how I am available to my mentee."	As your relationship evolves, your boundaries with your mentee will need to change. Use the guide to help foster the conversation.	**Boundary Setting** (see page 27)
"My mentee is having difficult feelings and I'm not sure how to help"	Encourage your student to identify their feelings using resources and encourage further conversation so that you can help them to find the right support.	**Feelings Wheel** (see page 53)

RESOURCES TO-GO

A growing collection of resources can be found by scanning the QR code below. Check back often as policies, tools, and resources evolve to meet the times.

ACKNOWLEDGMENTS

WE'D LIKE TO take this opportunity to acknowledge a few key people for their role in making this guide and our organization the success that they are.

First, our thanks to Dr. Brittany Clayborne for her significant contributions to the content of this guide. Thank you for approaching this project through the lens of both your psychology background and experience as a Mentors Care mentor.

Thank you to the entire Mentors Care team for helping build this incredible program that inspires mentors to be the best they can be for our students.

Throughout this guide you've heard about the importance of the coordinator role – for you, for our students, and our communities. These folks are generally handling lots of situations simultaneously. They are the connectors that pull everything together… between mentors and students as well as students and the school and professional resources. We hold deep respect and appreciation for the heart they bring to this work everyday.

A big thank you also goes out to Vistra. We appreciate your investment in this project and in the communities we serve.

Last, but certainly not least, thank you, dear mentor. Without you, none of this would be possible.

Made in the USA
Columbia, SC
21 October 2024